Alaska's 49 Flavorite Recipes
From the 49th State

Plus Kidz Korner, Kidz Tested Recipes and A-Z Alaska Geography

from the
SIMPLY ALASKAN SISTERS
cookbooks

ALASKA'S 49 FLAVORITE RECIPES FROM THE 49TH STATE Plus
Kidz Korner, Kidz Tested Recipes and A-Z Alaska Geography

ISBN: 978-1-57833-718-7

Library of Congress Control Number: 2018960858

First Printing December 2018

Book Design: Crystal Burrell, 𝕿𝖔𝖉𝖉 𝕮𝖔𝖒𝖒𝖚𝖓𝖎𝖈𝖆𝖙𝖎𝖔𝖓𝖘

Printed in China through **Alaska Print Brokers**, Anchorage, Alaska

Published by:
SIMPLY ALASKAN
SISTERS COOKBOOKS
P.O. Box 201172
Anchorage, Alaska 99520
www.simplyalaskansisters.com

Distributed by:

𝕿𝖔𝖉𝖉 𝕮𝖔𝖒𝖒𝖚𝖓𝖎𝖈𝖆𝖙𝖎𝖔𝖓𝖘
611 E. 12th Ave., Suite 102
Anchorage, Alaska 99501
Phone: (907) 274-TODD (8633) • Fax: (907) 929-5550
with other offices in Juneau and Fairbanks, Alaska
WWW.ALASKABOOKSANDCALENDARS.COM • sales@toddcom.com

RECIPE CONTENTS

To make your recipe truly outstanding use only the finest seafood available anywhere. Contact our friends at 10th and M Seafoods at 800-770-2722 or at www.10thandmseafoods.com. They also carry Alaska reindeer sausage used in several of our recipes.

Alaska's Flag Song
Eight stars of gold on a field of blue,
Alaska's flag, may it mean to you,
The blue of the sea, the evening sky,
The mountain lakes and the flowers nearby,
The gold of the early sourdough's dreams,
The precious gold of the hills and streams,
The brilliant stars in the northern sky,
The "Bear," the "Dipper," and shining high,
The great North Star with its steady light,
O'er land and sea a beacon bright,
Alaska's flag to Alaskans dear,
The simple flag of a last frontier.

Alaska Flag Fun Facts:
The flag is based on the design of Benny Benson, a thirteen year- old resident of the Jesse Lee Mission Home in Seward, Alaska. The Alaska Territorial Legislature adopted his design on May 2, 1927.

Marie Drake is credited with writing the words to Alaska's Flag song in 1935 which was written as a poem.

Elinor Dusenbury composed a song around the flag and poem in 1938.

The Territorial Legislature adopted the flag and song in 1955 and it became the official State flag and song when Alaska became the 49th State in 1959.

FOREWORD

It's all about timing, right?

Cindy Cheney Smirnoff and Barbara Cruz Stallone are long-time Alaskan residents. Cindy's family moved to the Kenai Peninsula in 1960 as commercial set-net fishermen.

Barb was born in the state's largest city, Anchorage. At that time, Alaska was a territory of the United States.

What makes us 'Sisters' is our 40 plus years of friendship and always sharing our culinary adventures and talents. "We should write a cookbook!"

From the Kenai Peninsula for Cindy and Anchorage Bowl/Big Lake for Barb, we share our childhood history from the country life to Alaska's largest city, Anchorage.

Our kitchens express our past lifestyles from albeit, often rock-n-roll cooking on the Bering Sea (*Deadliest Catch*), to NO electricity, no running water, mud and ice roads, outhouses to island living. We share each delicious creative recipe with a smile and say, "Welcome to our Alaska."

Warning, "We Brag about Alaska," wherever we travel and the amazing folks our trails cross, we share the amazing 'Aura of Alaska'.

Oh, always wanted to go to Alaska? Alaska's Gold Rush history and modern methods of transportation and communication keep Alaska on step with the OUTSIDE (meaning the Lower 48 states.)

All the TV and reality shows only depict some of the highlights of our Last Frontier.

Do not forget the 49th State is the most sparsely populated of all the states. The Panhandle of Alaska is just 746 miles from the State of Washington, separated by Canada. So, the kitchen moments and kids eager to help vary in each community. Simply Alaskan Sisters struggled to share only 49 special recipes because we are the 49th state in the U.S. We could have spouted proudly about our northern lights or the highest mountain in North America (Denali), or where we can even see Russia. But we chose to share our state in facts, fun and recipes for all ages, especially children, in our Kidz Korner section, and the Alaska state facts of A-Z Geography.

No matter what age, learning is contagious!

Thumb through our flavorite recipes, but most of all, sit back and discover more about Alaska, and bring along your kids to learn…children and grandchildren alike.

Welcome to the 49th and pages of our childhood state!

We dare you not to have fun exploring Alaska.

Simply Alaskan Sisters

Barb and Cindy

21,310 Feet High-Strawberry Pie
(Elevation of Denali)

This recipe makes an eye-popping dessert, that is a perfect pairing when you are looking for a dessert that is light, airy and full of flavor.

Ingredients
- Crust - Not rolled
- 1 ½ cups flour
- ½ cup oil
- 1 ½ tsp. sugar
- 2 tbsp. milk
- 1 tsp. salt

Directions
Mix all ingredients together in pie plate. Mix oil and milk together and pour into dry ingredients. Mix into ball and pat into pie pan to form crust. Push up the side of the pan to form into crust rim. Bake at 375 degrees for 12-15 minutes. Cool to room temperature before filling.

Strawberry Filling
- 2 egg whites
- 1 cup sugar
- 1 tbsp. lemon juice
- 1 small package frozen strawberries
- ½ pint whipping cream

Directions
2 egg whites beaten until foamy using an electric mixer. Add 1 cup sugar and 1 tbsp. lemon juice and strawberries that are nearly thawed. Beat mixture 15 minutes. Use a large bowl, as mixture expands a great deal. Use a glass or metal mixing bowl. Do not stop mixing until you have reached 15 minutes. Whip 1/2 pint whipping cream in a separate bowl and fold into egg white mixture. Pile into pre-baked and cooled pie crust. Freeze until ready to serve.

This pie will be VERY HIGH!

49th State Karat Cake

My Mother, Mildred Cruz, was a nurse at Providence Hospital in Anchorage for over 20 years, beginning in 1947, taking a break for children and returning in 1959 after the birth of my brother. This recipe was served at the hospital for many of the years she worked there and was a favorite of the doctors and nurses.

Serves up to 12. Bake at 325 degrees for 1 ½ hour.

Ingredients

- 3 cups sifted cake flour
- 2 cups sugar
- 2 tsp. cinnamon
- ½ tsp. soda
- ½ tsp. salt
- 1 tsp. baking powder
- 1 eight oz. can crushed pineapple
- 3 eggs, beaten together
- 1 ½ cups cooking oil
- 2 tsp. vanilla
- ½ cup raisins
- ½ cup coconut
- 2 cups grated raw carrot
- ½ cups chopped pecans

Directions

Mix together all of the dry ingredients. Drain pineapple, reserving syrup. Add pineapple syrup to dry mixture. Add eggs, cooking oil and vanilla. Beat three minutes. Stir in pineapple, nuts, carrots, raisins and coconut. Bake in a Bundt pan that has been sprayed with non-stick cooking spray with flour. Bake at 325 degrees for 1 ½ hour.

Glaze - let cake cool in pan for 10-15 minutes. Turn out on plate. Combine ¾ cup powdered sugar, ¼ cup grated carrots and 1 tbsp. lemon juice. Drizzle over cake.

Note: May bake in a 9 x 13 glass pan for about 1 hour. May frost with cream cheese icing for a change.

Alaska Snow Ball Melts (cookies)

These wonderful, melt-in-your-mouth cookies were passed down from Cindy's Polish grandparents.

Makes 4 dozen 1" round cookies. Bake at 400 degrees for 10 to 12 minutes.

Ingredients
- 2 sticks (1 cup) room-soft butter
- 2 tbsp. packed brown sugar
- 1 tsp. imitation vanilla
- ¼ tsp. table salt
- 2 ¼ cups flour
- ¾-1 cup chopped nuts (pecans or walnuts)
- ½ cup powdered sugar to coat and dust cookies

Directions
Mix butter, sugar and vanilla thoroughly in medium size mixing bowl, slowly adding flour, salt and nuts. Chill dough about 15 minutes.

Roll dough into 1 inch or smaller balls placing close on ungreased cookie sheets, they will not spread out.

Bake until set but not brown - about 10-12 minutes at 400 degrees.

While still warm roll each cookie in a bowl of powdered sugar. Set on sheets to cool. Roll cookies in the powdered sugar again for that extra 'snow' look.

Yum, melts in your mouth, not your hands.

* * *

Cookie Fun Fact:
Girl Scout cookies date back to 1917.

Bristol Bay Blueberry Coffee Cake

This is the coffee cake your grandmother made. Smells wonderful while baking and brings back all those childhood memories. Can be made in muffin tins if you prefer but I usually double this recipe and bake in a 9x13 inch glass pan.

Serves 9 3 inch squares. Bake at 375 degrees for 35-45 minutes if using an 8 inch square pan.

Ingredients
- ¾ cup sugar
- ¼ cup soft butter
- 1 egg
- ½ cup milk
- 2 cups flour
- 2 tsp. baking powder
- ½ tsp. salt
- 1 tsp. vanilla
- 2 cups blueberries

Topping:
- ½ cup brown sugar
- ½ cup flour
- 2 tsp. cinnamon
- ¼ cup soft butter

Directions
Mix butter, sugar and egg - beating thoroughly. Stir in milk. Add dry ingredients and stir into mixture. Gently stir in the blueberries so as not to turn batter blue. Spread batter into 8 inch square pan that has been sprayed with non-stick spray with flour. Spread mixed topping ingredients over the batter. Bake at 375 degrees for 35-45 minutes until toothpick inserted in middle comes out clean. If doubling this recipe, baking time will increase to 50-60 minutes.

Blueberry Fun Fact:
Blueberries freeze in just 4 minutes.

Peninsula Snowy White Crème Brûlée

Gather for an elegant easy dessert. If you are counting calories or serving a diabetic, use sugar-free pudding. Garnish with berries, mint or nuts.

Serves 6

Ingredients
- 2 boxes 3 oz. instant white chocolate pudding mix (may use cheesecake or vanilla)
- 1 ¾ cup milk
- 6 tsp. brown sugar for sprinkling on top

Directions
Add milk to pudding mix and whisk until slightly thickened. You may wish to add nuts, dried fruit or coconut to the pudding mix.

Pour into ramekins or similar type bowl and refrigerate for at least 1 hour.

When ready to serve gently sprinkle about 1 tsp brown sugar evenly over each dish.

Use a kitchen blow torch or hand-held fire starter to brown the sugar or be careful and use your oven broiler to caramelize the brown sugar. Watch carefully as it can burn quickly.

Return to refrigerator and let sit for a few minutes.

Your guests or family will love this dessert. Bon Appetit!

. . . .

Crème Brûlée Fun Fact:
First known usage dates back to 1691, wow now that is old!

Ruby Alaska Rhubarb-Berry Cobbler

This is a delicious cobbler that is best when served warm with a scoop of Vanilla Bean ice cream or a dollop of whipped cream and always brings rave reviews.

Serves up to 10 Bake: 50 minutes at 375 degrees

Ingredients

- 3 cups of fresh or frozen berries (thawed): strawberries, blueberries, raspberries, or blackberries.
- 2 cups fresh or frozen rhubarb (thawed)
- 1 ¼ cup granulated sugar
- 3 tbsp. lemon juice
- 1 ¼ cup flour, divided
- 1 tsp. cinnamon or nutmeg

Toppings:

- ½ cup uncooked quick-cooking oats
- ½ cup packed brown sugar
- ½ cup cold butter, cut into small pieces

Directions

Combine first four ingredients in a bowl. Add ¼ cup flour, coating fruit and stir. Pour mixture into a 9x13 inch pan, coating first with non-stick cooking spray.

Topping

Combine oats, brown sugar and remaining flour in a small bowl; cut in cold butter with a fork or pastry blender until mixture resembles coarse crumbs. Sprinkle mixture over fruit filling.

Bake at 375 degrees for 45 to 50 minutes.

Note: may use peaches, frozen or thawed, or other stone fruit in combination with rhubarb. For diabetics' substitute sugar for agave, stevia or other sugar substitute.

Ruby Alaska Rhubarb - Berry Cobbler

Rhubarb Fun Fact
DO <u>NOT</u> eat the leaf, stock only!
The leaves of Rhubard are
poisonous!

13

ALASKA'S 49 FLAVORITE RECIPES

Kachemak Crab, Capers and Artichoke Dip

This is a versatile dip that can be used to serve as a topping for halibut, cod or salmon. You can also stuff shrimp which makes a beautiful presentation. Additionally, you may want to use it as a salad spread on an open-faced sandwich or even put it in your omelet.

Serves 6-8

Ingredients
- ¼ cup sour cream
- 2 10 oz. jars of artichokes drained and chopped
- ½ cup mayonnaise
- 4 oz. cream cheese softened
- ½ cup sweet onion diced
- 1 ½ cup crab meat (for the BEST crab ever, check out 10th and M Seafoods)
- ½ cup parmesan cheese (reserve 3 tbsp. to sprinkle on top)
- ¼ cup capers
- 2 tbsp. parsley chopped
- 1 tbsp. Tabasco or other hot sauce
- Salt and white pepper to taste
- Seasoned bread crumbs

Directions
Mix sour cream, mayonnaise and cream cheese together. Add artichokes, onion, parmesan cheese, capers, parsley, salt and pepper and mix. Add Tabasco and crab and mix thoroughly. Spread in a casserole dish and cover with seasoned bread crumbs and the 3 tbsp. of parmesan cheese. Bake at 350 degrees for 15-20 minutes until the top is lightly browned.

This is a wonderful appetizer for any meal.

· ·

Artichoke Fun Fact:
It actually is an unbloomed flower, part of the sunflower family.

Matanuska Vege Mock Guac'

Growing up on the Kenai Peninsula, if you could find a good avocado you were lucky. If you are out of avocados or they are not in season or just too expensive, this recipe is a life saver! You can be as creative as your heart desires with seasonings and add-ons.

Serves 4-6 as a dip with your flavorite chip or vegetables.

Ingredients
- 2 cups frozen peas
- ½ cup sour cream
- ¼ cup finely diced red onion and or green onions
- 2 cloves of fresh garlic diced
- ¼ cup finely diced sweet bell pepper
- 1 can green mild chilies
- Juice of 2-3 medium limes
- Salt to taste

Directions
Blend all above ingredients together to make the consistency of a dip.

A food processor or blender work best!

Be creative and add your favorite spices, such as garlic powder, cumin, taco seasoning, pepitas or pomegranate arils.

Hint: *Extra spices are best!*

Refrigerate and serve with vegetables or chips.

Mini Dutch Harbor Crab Cakes

We have eaten crab cakes all over the world. Although they are always a little different variation, these are our favorite. For the BEST always use Alaskan King or Dungeness Crab. We highly recommend 10th and M Seafoods at www.10thandmseafoods.com or call 800-770-2722, for the finest seafood anywhere on the planet.

Serves 8

Ingredients *Aioli:*
- 2 cups mayonnaise
- 3 garlic cloves finely chopped
- Juice of 1 lemon
- ½ tsp. salt
- Dash of Asian hot chili sauce
- ½ bunch of tarragon, parsley or cilantro finely chopped

Crab Cakes:
- 1½ pounds crab meat
- ¾ cup bread crumbs or panko, plus additional crumbs for coating
- 2 green onions finely chopped
- Olive oil

Directions

Mix all aioli in a medium sized bowl and set aside.

Combine crab meat, bread crumbs and onions in another bowl. Add about ½ cup aioli, just enough to hold loosely together and stir.

Form into 8 cakes about 3 inches in diameter. Coat one side only with crumbs and set aside.

Heat olive oil in a sauté pan over medium high heat. Place cakes in pan crumb side down. Sauté until golden brown, 3-4 minutes. Use your spatula to turn over carefully. Turn down heat to medium low and sauté until heated through, 3-4 additional minutes.

Keep warm in a 150-degree oven until finished sautéing all the cakes. Top with aioli just before serving with a slice of lemon, cocktail sauce or tartar sauce.

These are always the hit of the party at any gathering!

Sassy Seward Crab and Shrimp Spread

This recipe is shared by Lee Winfree, one of the owners of 10th and M Seafoods. She says she triples this recipes and shares with her family and friends as it is a favorite of everyone. Purchase your seafood at 10th and M Seafoods. Call 800-770-2722 or order from their website www.10thandmseafoods.com.

Ingredients

- 1 lb. crab meat (snow or king crab) or ½ lb. crab and ½ lb. small shrimp)
- 1 cup mayonnaise
- ½ cup sour cream
- 1 8 oz. package cream cheese
- 3 drops of soy sauce
- 1 tbsp. Worcestershire
- ¼ plus tbsp. Tabasco
- Dash of cayenne
- Salt to taste
- 2 large garlic cloves minced
- 2 green onions thinly sliced

Directions

Drain seafood in a colander for at least one hour. Soften cream cheese. Mix all ingredients except seafood, blend until creamy and smooth. Stir in crab or crab and shrimp and green onion with a fork.

Lee always adds extra Tabasco and makes a day ahead of time when she wants to serve this succulent dip.

Your family and friends will want you to share this fabulous recipe, so they too can enjoy with their friends.

Who can resist a great seafood dip?

Valley Jalapeño Cheddar Butter

Classy looking spread, fast and easy - get your cheese fix!

Ingredients
- 1 cup coarsely grated cheddar cheese
- 1 cup coarsely grated pepper jack cheese
- 1 tbsp. corn starch
- ¼ cup minced mild jalapeños (pickled or fresh)
- ¼ cup minced green onions
- miscellaneous minced sweet peppers
- horseradish to taste
- ½ cup sour cream and/or mayonnaise for texture

Directions
Mix cheeses and corn starch in separate bowl coating cheeses with corn starch. In a medium bowl mix jalapeño, green onions, sweet peppers, horseradish, sour cream and/or mayonnaise. Add grated cheese to the mixture stirring gently. Increase the horseradish to your taste. You may substitute a hot sauce for horseradish if you prefer. If you like a warmer taste, use hot jalapeños to get that zing. Try diced green chilis for even more taste. This recipe is easily adapted to what is in your cupboard.

Alaska Reindeer Sausage Gumbo

Most Alaskans came here from another state. During the building of the trans-Alaska pipeline many workers came from Louisiana. They brought their love of gumbo with them and this recipe has been adapted to use Alaskan reindeer sausage and shrimp. If you are not a true gumbo aficionado do not add the heat, cayenne pepper, and you will still have a wonderful dish.

Serves 8

Ingredients

- ½ cup vegetable or canola oil
- ¾ cup flour
- 1 sweet onion chopped medium fine
- 2 stalks celery diced
- 1 green, yellow, orange or red bell pepper diced
- 4-6 garlic cloves chopped
- 1-2 bay leaves
- 6 cups chicken broth
- 1 cup Alaskan reindeer sausage minced (can use mild or hot)
- 2 chicken breasts cooked, cooled and diced
- ½ lb. medium shrimp, cut in half or quarters
- 2 cups steamed rice
- ¼ cup sliced green onions

Gumbo Seasoning

- 1 tsp. dried basil
- Black pepper to taste
- White pepper to taste
- 1 tsp. cayenne pepper
- Corn starch for thickening

Directions

Use a black cast iron skillet, if you have one. If not, you can always use a non-stick skillet.

Heat skillet over a medium heat, add flour and oil to make the roux. Stir continually until flour browns.

In another pot cook celery and onion until translucent. Add roux, chicken stock, garlic, bay leaf, chicken and sausage. Bring to a boil and simmer for 1 hour. May need to skim the foam off. Add shrimp about 15 minutes before serving as shrimp cook very quickly.

Season to taste with your gumbo seasoning adding a little at a time. As always, a little goes a long way.

Note: if you do not have reindeer sausage, you may substitute other types such as kielbasa.

21

'For the Halibut' Chowder

(see back page cover photo)

This recipe has been adapted from a variety of similar recipes. There is nothing better on a cold day than to come home and have a bowl of halibut chowder. Warms your insides like none other, and with a slice of warm bread or a warm biscuit you will see why this is one of our favorites.

Serves 6-8

Ingredients

- 2 cans cream of chicken soup
- 1 can cream of mushroom soup
- 2 cups milk
- 1 cup chicken broth or clam broth
- 1 pkg. frozen corn
- 1 8 oz. pkg. cream cheese
- 2 lbs. halibut or cod chunks
- 6 green onions sliced
- 1 clove garlic finely minced
- ½ cup chopped celery
- ½ cup chopped carrots (optional)
- ½ green bell pepper chopped
- ½ red, orange or yellow bell pepper chopped
- ¼ tsp. red pepper flakes (optional)

Directions

Sauté onions, garlic, celery, carrots, green and red pepper in 1/3 stick of butter. Add halibut and sauté until chunks flake. Add to soup mixture including cream cheese which has been slowly dissolved into the soup mixture. You can add extra soup and milk to make this recipe stretch further.

Note: I have added other seafood to this recipe such as shrimp, clams, scallops and crab to make this a seafood chowder. Your friends and family will rave about this dish and it is so easy to make. Serve in a large bowl with some parsley garnish or paprika on top. Yum!

(See back cover photo)

Mighty Moose Meat Chili

If you don't have moose meat, use lean ground beef, ground chicken or turkey. Will taste just as good as the seasonings are what makes a great chili. On a chilly winter day, a bowl of chili with a slice of warm bread, just out of the oven, will warm your insides as well as your heart.

Serves 4-6

Ingredients

- 1 lb. moose meat (ground beef, ground chicken, ground turkey or ground sausage)
- 1 cup chopped onion
- 1 clove garlic crushed
- ½ tsp. salt
- 3 tsp. or more to taste of chili powder
- ¼ tsp. pepper
- 2 tsp. cumin
- 3 cups canned tomatoes diced
- 1 6 oz. can of tomato paste

Optional

- 2 cans 16oz. kidney beans undrained
- 1 can 4 oz. chopped green chiles undrained

Directions

Brown meat and onion in a medium skillet and drain. In a large pot, combine remaining ingredients including ground meat mixture. Bring to a boil stirring the pot frequently so that nothing sticks to the bottom. Reduce heat to a simmer, cover pot and cook for 2 hours, stirring occasionally. Serve in a bowl topped with grated cheese and diced onions. Can be made the day ahead or frozen for later use.

Northern Cioppino
(Succulent Seafood Bowls)

Pronounced –'Chuh-PEE-noh'
Steamy bowls of extravagant seafood swimming in a savory sauce of gentle flavors. Do all your seafood shopping at www.10thandmseafoods. com or call them at 800-770-2722.

Serves 6

Ingredients

- Use a variety of Alaskan seafood such as listed below
- 1 lb. skinned halibut or cod - cut into bite size pieces
- 2 lbs. of medium mussels in unopened shells. Scrubbed VERY clean
- 3 lbs. (3-4 whole legs) of cleaned/cooked king crab or Dungeness crab legs, broken at the joints
- 2 lbs. of raw medium size shrimp with shells
- 2 lbs. of raw scallops, medium size
- 4 green onions diced
- 1 green pepper diced

- 5 garlic cloves diced
- 2 celery stalks diced
- 1 yellow or white onion diced
- 3 cans of 14.5 oz. tomatoes diced with juice (Italian or Mexican)
- 2 cups of V-8 vegetable juice.
- 4 cups of chicken or vegetable broth (full bodied flavor)
- 2 bay leaves (remove from broth before serving)
- 4 basil leaves chopped for garnish

Optional seasonings to taste: *Salt pepper, cumin, curry, etc.*

Remember taste and stir. This succulent sauce is the sensational part of your Cioppino. (Directions on next page)

Directions (Northern Cioppino)

Use a large stock pot which will hold over 10-12 cups and lots of seafood.

Sauté all the vegetables in 1-2 tbs. of olive oil for 3-5 minutes in the stock pot. Add the cans of tomatoes, V-8 juice and broth. Add bay leaves and simmer for 45 minutes. Taste test. Your sauce should be a hardy soup consistency. Remember, you can add flavors, as you taste. Take your time to create this amazing succulent sauce.

The seafood is added just before you serve your Cioppino. Plan at least 20-30 minutes before serving. Taste!

Raise your savory sauce from simmer to med-hot temperature, stirring often. Add washed cool seafood in this order.

Halibut and mussels, cook 5-8 minutes. Taste test. Mussels should be opening. Taste test. Add the shrimp and crab parts, 3-5 min. then the scallops last, cooking 3-5 minutes longer.

Serve in large bowls, garnish with chopped basil and a dash of parmesan cheese.

(dollop of sour cream optional)

Note: Cioppino Is a finely tuned process. Do not be in a hurry. The savory broth is the important base. Be creative, add a touch of hot sauce.

Serve with our 'Forget-Me-Not' biscuits to dip in broth/sauce.

Try our Cook Inlet Sweet & Sour Cucumber Salad to accompany.

(Recipe ingredients photo on the front cover.)

Dessert: Ooops, you should have served dessert first! Remember?
But, try our 21,310 Feet High Strawberry Pie!
Dine, Alaskan Style. Say 'Bueno'

Salmon Caesar Salad

Are you looking for a quick and healthy dinner for your family? We should all try to eat more wild Alaska salmon. This easy recipe can be done and on the table in a matter of minutes. Use smoked salmon, canned salmon or leftover salmon that wasn't finished from last weeks' meal that you froze because you knew you didn't want to throw away good food. (Besides your parents always told you about those children who were starving, and that was why you needed to clean your plate).

Serves 4

Ingredients

- 2 cups cold flaked salmon (ensure all pin bones are removed)
- 2 diced green onions, finely chopped
- 4 hardboiled eggs, quartered
- 4 -5 cups torn romaine lettuce, washed
- 2 cups cherry tomatoes, halved (optional)
- 1 cup sliced cucumber (optional)
- 2 cups grated Parmesan cheese, or Pecorino Romano
- Croutons, either store bought or homemade if you have the time
- Salt and pepper to taste

Dressing

- 5 anchovy fillets or 2-3 tbsp. of anchovy paste
- 2-3 garlic cloves
- 2 tbsp. Dijon mustard
- 3 tbsp red wine vinegar
- 1 tbsp. lemon juice
- Salt and pepper to taste
- ½ cup grated Parmesan or Pecorino Romano Cheese
- ½ cup olive oil

Directions

Place torn romaine lettuce in bowl, add salmon, green onions and any other vegetables you would like. Sprinkle cheese over the salad. Salad dressing should be mixed in a blender or mini-prep processor, so all ingredients are thoroughly mixed. Spoon over the salad mixture and top with croutons. Garnish with hard boiled eggs and a sprig of dill or parsley.

Note: This dish may be served as a salad or entrée.

Wasilla Watermelon Rock Salad

So many watermelon ways to please!

Ingredients
- One ripe medium size seedless watermelon
- 6 fresh basil leaves
  and/or
- Cilantro leaves

Directions
Try serving this salad from the watermelon itself. Make it your bowl.

Cut the watermelon either in half or lengthwise. Use a one-inch melon baller and carefully 'ball' out entire halves. Not too close to the wall, leave a sweet red color on the watermelon walls. Cover the watermelon halves and refrigerate.

Place the watermelon balls in a separate bowl. Using kitchen scissors, roll up the basil and or cilantro, thin cut strips. Add the herbs to the bowl of watermelon balls.

Place watermelon balls and herbs into a zip lock back and refrigerate until time to plate.

Plating the watermelon uses your creativity. Add whole fresh berries, or wedges of available fruit.

No seeds to spit, but empty bowls to fill. With extra watermelon juice, freeze and use as ice cubes.

Do the Watermelon Rock Dance! So pretty to serve and so delicious to eat.

Cook Inlet Sweet & Sour Cucumber Salad

Cucumber fans, this is so popular, folks will even drink the juice.

Serves 4-6

Ingredients

- 3 medium size cucumbers or two English cucumbers
- 1 cup white sugar
- ½ cup white vinegar
- ½ cup warm water
- ¼ cup finely diced green onions
- ¼ cup thin sliced radishes and or sweet peppers

Directions

- Take a 4-cup measuring cup (prefer glass)
- Pour in sugar to 1 cup
- Add vinegar to 1 ½ cup
- Add water to two cups

Mix well till all sugar has dissolved and liquid is clear. Place liquid in a new zip lock bag and add the sliced cucumbers, onions etc. Seal the zip-lock bag and place in fridge for a least one hour. Serve with juice drained and saved. Add a garnish to the cucs and serve with a slotted spoon.

Be ready for oohs and ahhs!

Russian River Raspberry Slaw

There are an abundance of vegetables and wild berries flourishing on the Kenai Peninsula. This is an excellent way to get fruit and roughage on your menu.

Ingredients
- 5 cups shredded cabbage/ mixed colors with carrots
- 1 cup of fresh raspberries (may use strawberries or other berries)
- 3 tbsp. mayonnaise
- ¼ tsp. pepper
- ¼ tsp. salt
- 1 tsp. red wine vinegar (add celery seeds or other to taste)

Directions
Place the mixed shredded cabbage and ½ cup raspberries in a large bowl. Mix mayonnaise, salt/pepper and vinegar together and blend in cabbage.

Make more mayonnaise mix if cabbage is not completely mixed and moist.

Refrigerate, covered 15-20 min.

Serve in a complementary bowl with remaining ½ cup raspberries on top for garnish.

This makes a beautiful presentation and is a healthy complement to any dinner!

Raspberry Fun Fact:
They come in all sorts of colors, but the gold ones are the sweetest!

Baked Willow Ptarmigan Breasts

The ptarmigan is the state bird of Alaska. If you do not have ptarmigan you may substitute chicken breasts and chicken thighs, so you have a combination of white and dark meat. This recipe is excellent served with mashed or boiled potatoes, or rice if you prefer.

Serves 4-6

Ingredients

- 3 boneless ptarmigan breasts or chicken breasts
- 3 boneless ptarmigan thighs or chicken thighs
- ¼ cup butter with 3 tbsp. oil
- 1 ½ cup flour
- 1 tsp. salt
- ½ tsp. pepper
- 1 tsp. dried parsley
- Half of onion chopped fine
- 2 ½ cups chicken stock
- ½ cup sweet basil leaves chopped

Directions

Dip Ptarmigan or chicken in flour mixed with salt, pepper and thyme. Brown slowly in butter and oil in a deep skillet on the stove. Add onions toward the end of the browning process and cook until translucent. Add chicken stock and basil, cover and cook slowly on low heat for about 2 hours or until very tender. Add more chicken broth if it cooks down. Strain sauce and thicken slightly with corn starch mixed with a little cold water. Pour over ptarmigan or chicken to serve. Garnish with a sprig of parsley.

Note: Excellent served over boiled or mashed potatoes or rice.

* *

Ptarmigan Fun Fact:

They fly into snow banks so they don't leave tracks, to make it harder for predators to find them.

Chicken, Alaska: Finger Lickin' Good Chicken

As a child growing up in Anchorage this was one of our favorite recipes. The warm gravy on a cold winter day tasted so good and the smell coming from the oven was to die for.

Serves 6

Ingredients
- 2 ½ lbs. fryer or your favorite parts
- ¼ cup butter
- ½ cup flour
- ½ tsp. salt
- ¼ tsp. pepper
- ½ tsp. paprika
- 2 cans cream of chicken soup
- 1-2 4 oz. cans of sliced mushrooms
- 1 16 oz. can cooked onions
- 2 tbsp. chopped pimento
- 1 tbsp. chopped parsley
- ¼ cup dry sherry cooking wine or white wine

Directions
Cut chicken into parts or use the purchased parts. Dry on paper towel. Use a gallon zip lock bag to hold flour, salt, pepper and paprika. Dredge chicken parts in the flour mixture. Melt butter in a 9x13 baking dish and place chicken skin side up. Do not turn. Bake 30 minutes at 400 degrees.

Heat chicken soup, onions and juice, mushrooms with juice, pimento, parsley and sherry to boiling in a sauce pan on the stove.

Turn chicken over and pour sauce over it.

Bake 35-45 minutes longer.

Serve with biscuits, vegetable and a salad.

Yummy!

Alaska Moose Comfort Food

If you already have a favorite meat loaf recipe, you can pass this one by. If you are still looking for an outstanding recipe, you must try this one. It is a never fail and always fits the bill.

Serves 6-8 Bake at 350 degrees

Ingredients

- 1 cup milk
- 1 cup diced onions
- 6 slices bread
- 2 lbs. moose meat, lean ground beef, ground chicken or ground turkey
- 1 cup grated cheese (pecorino romano or parmesan)
- ½ tsp. salt
- ¼ tsp. pepper
- ¼ cup dried parsley
- 2 to 4 garlic cloves minced
- 4 eggs beaten

- ½ cup ketchup
- cup brown sugar
- 1 tsp. mustard
- 1 tsp. Worcestershire sauce
- *Optional*: dash of hot sauce

Directions

Tear the bread into bite size pieces. Pour the milk over the

Topping:

bread and allow to soak for 10-20 minutes. In a large mixing bowl put the meat, onions, bread soaked in milk, cheese, salt, pepper, parsley, garlic and eggs. Be sure your hands are clean, mix the ingredients until everything is combined.

Shape the mixture on a foil lined broiling pan.

Mix the ingredients for your topping together in a bowl and pour ½ over the top of the meat.

Bake at 350 degrees for 45 minutes, and then pour the remaining sauce over the meat. Bake another 20 to 25 minutes and remove from oven. The meat should not be pink in the center. Let the meat loaf rest for 10 minutes.

Serve with a green salad and you have a healthy and delicious dinner.

Tundra Pork Medallions
~ala~ Fairbanks Fried Rice

Who doesn't like pork medallions? This recipe is so easy, even your children can help with the preparation. Can be either grilled on the bar-b-que, baked in the oven or fried in a pan on the stove.

Serves: 4

Ingredients

- 1 lb. pork tenderloin trimmed cut into 1-inch slices
- 1 tbsp. lemon juice
- 1/3 cup sesame oil
- 1/3 cup rice vinegar
- 2 tbsp. brown sugar
- 2 cloves of garlic minced
- Ground black pepper to taste
- ½ tsp. salt

Directions

In a gallon zip lock plastic bag mix all ingredients. Close zip lock and place in the refrigerator for at least 2 hours.

Remove the meat from the marinade.

Cook on a medium grill or in the oven at 400 degrees for 20-25 minutes, until a meat thermometer reaches 170 degrees or fry in a non-stick frying pan on medium heat until the medallions are no longer pink in the center. Serve with our Alaskan Fried Rice.

See recipe for FAIRBANKS FRIED RICE is Nice!

Alaska Reindeer Sausage Pizza

If your family loves pizza as much as mine, you will love this recipe. My mother started making pizza for us in the 1950's, long before the franchises became popular. We make our own crust, sometimes buy canned pizza sauce or use homemade marinara. My kids loved cold pizza the next day for breakfast or warmed up in the microwave.

Serves 4-6 Makes 12 pieces so serving depends on how many you eat.

Ingredients
Crust-
- 1 pkg. yeast
- ¼ cup lukewarm water
- ½ tsp. salt
- ¼ cup olive oil
- ¾ cup warm water
- 2 cups or a little more flour
- If you like a thicker crust add 1 tsp. sugar and let dough rise in mixing bowl for 30 minutes in a warm spot

Topping-
- 1 ring Alaska Reindeer Sausage sliced
- 1 lb. mild sausage, lean ground beef, ground chicken or ground turkey
- 1 medium can sliced black olives
- fresh or canned sliced mushrooms
- slices of red, orange, yellow or green pepper
- 12 slices provolone cheese or 1 bag of your favorite pizza blend cheese

(Directions on the next page)

Directions (Alaska Reindeer Sausage Pizza)

Crust-

Dissolve yeast in ¼ cup warm water (not hot). Dissolve salt in ¾ cup warm water with olive oil added. Mix 2 cups flour, or a little more with yeast, and olive oil water. Mix with a knife or fork until a soft ball is formed. You may use a little corn meal on the cookie sheet before you spread dough. Put a little olive oil on your hands and spread dough on a large cookie sheet. Using your hands spread the dough to the edges of the cookie sheet. If you like a thicker crust, use a smaller cookie sheet or a round pizza pan.

Spread marinara or canned pizza sauce on the dough. Top with slices of reindeer sausage, other meats, olives, mushrooms, peppers and finally cheese. Use a little paprika around the edge of pizza with a little dried parsley flakes or a little oregano.

Bake at 425 degrees for 20-25 minutes until the crust is brown. To check on doneness, lift the corner of the pizza off the pan with a spatula to ensure the dough is baked all the way through.

• •

Pizza Fun Fact:

In 2001, Pizza Hut became the first restaurant chain to deliver to space. It was delivered to Yuri Usachov.

Fairbanks Fried Rice

So easy and uses the bits and pieces of vegetables in your fridge. Very kid friendly, and a super accompaniment with any dish.

Ingredients
- 1 cup rice, regular or instant (Try wild rice or other varieties.)
- ½ onion diced (red is pretty)
- 2 green onions diced
- ½ cup sweet peppers, (colors are fun) diced
- ½ cup frozen green peas
- 3 large eggs whipped
- cilantro or basil as garnishes
- soy sauce
- salt and pepper
- 1 chicken bouillon cube
- 1 tsp. butter

Directions
Cook the rice according to bag or box directions. Add one chicken bouillon cube and 1 tsp. butter to rice water. When cooking is complete, set aside in mixing bowl. Sauté in butter all the vegetables until al dente (semi crisp). Mix the eggs with ¼ cup water, milk or club soda. Scramble eggs until light and fluffy. Mix the rice, vegetables, and eggs together lightly. Return to pan and gently brown. Add soy sauce to taste, salt and pepper. Serve with our 'Tundra Tenderloin' recipe or our other main course!

Use a separate serving dish, with garnishes. Very colorful.

TIP: for extra nice presentation, use a 1 cup measuring cup and place rice inside and gently pack. Tip onto your main dinner plate with a sprig of garnish. Bon Appetit!

49th State Bean Parade

I have taken this recipe to many functions and it always receives rave reviews. You can delete the ground meat and it is still a great dish. If you add the ground meat, it can be used as an entrée. The taste will improve if made the day before.

Serves 6   Bake at350 degrees for 45 minutes

Ingredients
- 1 medium onion chopped
- 6 slices bacon chopped
- 1 lb. lean ground beef, turkey, chicken or sausage
- 1 can butter beans
- 1 can kidney beans
- 1 can pork and beans
- ½ cup brown sugar
- ½ cup white sugar
- 1 tbsp. cider vinegar
- ½ cup catsup
- 1 tsp. mustard

Directions
Cook bacon and remove from pan. Chop into small pieces. Add onion to hot bacon oil and cook until tender. Add ground meat and brown. Drain any fat from pan and add cooked bacon. Drain and rinse the butter and kidney beans. Add to the bacon, onions, and drained ground meat. Mix the pork and beans, sugar (white and brown), vinegar, catsup and mustard. Bake at 350 degrees for 45 minutes. Enjoy!

Delta Barley-Sausage Casserole Dressing

Growing up on the Kenai Peninsula was often a challenge as my mother, Loretta Cheney, couldn't just run to the grocery store if she was out of something. Many times, she created this dish from items left in her pantry.

To this day, folks just ask for Mrs. C's Barley Dish…

Serves 6-8

Ingredients

- 2 cups barley
- 1 cup minced celery
- 1 cup minced onions
- 1 can diced water chestnuts
- 2 – 3 medium eggs whipped
- 1 lb. breakfast or Italian sausage
- 1 cup sliced fresh mushrooms
- 2 tsp. ground sage or poultry spice
- 1 tsp. oregano or Italian spices
- 1 tsp. fresh ground pepper

Directions

Cook the barley per directions on package. We recommend adding a chicken bouillon cube and 1 tsp. butter to water. Do not overcook, al denté is delightful.

Place cooked barley in a large mixing bowl and cool.

Add all the diced, minced and sliced items and mix thoroughly. Add spices, then the whipped eggs. Blend everything completely and place in an oven-proof buttered casserole dish.

Bake at 350 degrees for 45-50 minutes until firm and browned on top.

Serve with beef, pork chops, turkey, chicken or our ptarmigan breast recipe in this book.

Did you know grains are king in the Delta Junction Valley? Not far from Fairbanks, barley production grows as Alaska continues to diversify its economic base.

Mystery Vege' Soufflé

Do not tell your guests this secret vegetable recipe, as it is so popular they will ask for the mystery dish.

Serves 6-8

Ingredients
- 7-8 cups of chopped fresh carrots
- 1 tsp. baking powder
- 1 tsp. vanilla extract
- ¼ tsp. salt
- 2 tbsp. melted butter
- 2/3 cup white sugar
- 3 tbsp. flour
- ¼ cup sour cream
- 3 large eggs
- 1 tsp. powdered sugar

Directions
Cook carrots in boiling water about 25 minutes until tender, drain. In a food processor or use a mixer, beat until smooth.

Add all other ingredients, mixing in eggs last. Mix well. Pour into a 2-quart casserole dish, sprayed with non-stick spray.

Bake at 350 degrees about 50-60 minutes until puffed and set. May sprinkle with powdered sugar before serving.

Often our kidz ask for this dish as dessert. Vegetables for dessert? What a testimony!

Valley Zucchini Casserole

If you like zucchini, you will love this and so will your family. An easy way for kidz to get their vegetables.

Serves 6

Ingredients
- 4 medium zucchinis grated or chopped
- 4 tbsp. butter melted
- ¾ cup shredded carrots
- ½ cup chopped onion
- 2 ¼ cup herbed stuffing cubes
- 1 can cream of chicken soup not diluted
- ½ cup sour cream

Directions
Mix all ingredients together in a bowl. Pour into a greased casserole dish. Bake for 30-40 minutes at 350 degrees.

Zucchini Fun Fact:
(Pronounced ZOO-KEE-NEE originally from Italy) Eaten both raw and cooked and the flower that blooms is edible. Zucchini can weigh over 1,500 lbs. and over 99 inches in length.

ALASKA'S 49 FLAVORITE RECIPES

10th & M Seafoods - A Brief History

Kroesing Cold Storage 1950's

10th & M Seafoods is rich in Alaskan history stemming from a humble beginning that started long before Alaska's statehood. Leo and Emilia Kroesing, to supplement their income, began raising mink and in 1938 Leo traded their mink pelts for a patch of land on 10th Avenue where he built their business, complete with a small cold storage building. Unfortunately, the noise from the military's P-38s landing at the adjacent strip (Delaney Park Strip) caused severe stress upon the mink, causing them to kill their young and all but destroying their new business. Leo and Emilia persevered by expanding their cold storage facility and Kroesing Cold Storage was born. Demand for cold storage was undeniable. Homesteaders and businesses were eager to take advantage of such a rare commodity. Until their retirement in 1960, Leo and Emilia also provided other invaluable services to their community, such as subsistence and sport caught fish and game processing.

After Leo retired, Kroesing Cold Storage was purchased and operated by Lu and Madeline Norene, who changed the name to 10th & M Lockers. Much of the original business model remained, but the new owners decided to expand the building in the early 1960's to include a small retail storefront. 10th & M Lockers rolled along until 1979 when a determined young businessman named Skip Winfree and his wife Lee purchased the company. Skip and Lee changed the business name again to convey their new strategy and 10th & M Seafoods was up and running. Skip used his background in corporate sales and marketing to reach out to local restaurant owners and chefs, major retail chains, military commissaries and North Slope catering companies to establish the company's new wholesale seafood distribution program.

Tourism within the state was growing rapidly. Skip and Lee realizing visitors were eager to take Alaskan seafood home with them, developed revolutionary packaging methods that allowed customers to carry their purchases with them on the airlines. Skip saw the bigger picture and 10th & M became the first seafood company in Alaska to offer door to door overnight air shipments to consumers around the country. It began through a relationship 10th & M developed with the International airfreight company Flying Tigers which was soon bought out by a rapidly growing company called Federal Express. Executives with FedEx were so impressed with the program that Skip and his team had put together that they invited them to the headquarters in Memphis to teach their team the concepts of packaging and shipping perishable goods around the world. Today, some thirty plus years later, this relationship has had a huge impact on not only 10th & M Seafoods and FedEx, but for countless companies around the world who now ship perishable goods to consumers everywhere.

From their humble beginnings to where they are today, 10th & M Seafoods has always been about Alaska and Alaskans first. They are proud to be a part of their community and to have secured a place in its history. The future lies with the next generation, with son Rob proudly taking the helm.

10th & M Seafoods today

Baked Halibut Denali

You will find many halibut recipes, but I doubt you will find one you like better than this. Halibut is a white fish with very little flavor, so it is important to dress it up. It will also dry out when overbaked so watch it carefully when in the oven.

Serves 6   Bake at 350 degrees for 18-20 minutes
(bake 10 minutes for each inch of filet)

Ingredients
- 2 lbs. halibut fillets
- ½ cup sour cream
- ½ cup mayonnaise
- ½ cup grated parmesan cheese
- Zest of a half lemon
- Dash of hot sauce (optional)
- ½ tsp. Dijon mustard
- ¼ of large onion diced
- Ritz crackers crushed (2 per serving)

Directions
Wash your fillets and pat dry on both sides. Place in a glass pan that has been sprayed with non-stick cooking spray. In a bowl mix sour cream, mayonnaise and parmesan cheese. Add lemon zest, hot sauce if desired, Dijon mustard. Mix well. Dice the onions and add to the mixture. Spread over the halibut fillets. Crushed crackers are then spread over the mixture.

Bake at 350 degrees for 18-20 minutes.

Bering Sea Bacon-Wrapped Scallops

Scallops are so easy to prepare, yet most cooks shy away from them because they are perceived as being difficult. You will love this recipe as it is simple and easy to prepare and always tastes soooo good.

Serves 4 (3-4 scallops per person) Bake at 425 degrees for 12-15 minutes

Ingredients
- 12-16 medium size scallops
- ½ slice thin cut bacon per scallop
- Olive oil for drizzling on top of scallops
- Salt, white pepper, garlic and paprika for both top and bottom of scallops

Directions
Pat scallops dry with a paper towel. Wrap scallop with 1/2 slice bacon and secure with a toothpick. Drizzle olive oil on the top and bottom of each scallop. Season with a little salt, white pepper, garlic and paprika on each side of the scallop.

Arrange scallops on a baking sheet sprayed with non-stick cooking oil or lined with parchment paper.

Bake at 425 degrees for 12-15 minutes.

Bush Baked Alaska Salmon

There are almost as many salmon recipes as the population of Alaska. The population in 2015 was 738,432, so I am slightly exaggerating. However, salmon is one of the staples of the Alaskan diet, so every family undoubtedly has a favorite way to fix salmon.

There are five species of salmon- pink or humpy, sockeye or red, chum or dog, coho or silver and chinook or king. It is hard to beat wild Alaskan salmon, so the following recipe is probably best served using sockeye, coho or king salmon.

Ingredients
- 3-5 cloves of fresh garlic
- 2 tbsp. of lemon juice
- ¼ cup butter melted
- 1 filet of fresh Alaska salmon

Directions
Take a piece of tin foil larger than your filet and fold up the sides, so garlic lemon butter does not run off. Place filet skin side down on tin foil.

Use a spoon to spread the melted butter, lemon juice and garlic liberally over the filet.

Place on your bar-b-que at a medium heat for approximately 12 minutes, until salmon is done. The salmon meat should not be translucent but pink all the way through. Cooking time depends on the thickness of the filet. Usually 10 minutes per inch of thickness of filet.

To serve, place tin foil on a cookie sheet. Slide a spatula between salmon skin and the salmon meat and slide under the salmon. Place on a pretty plate with lemon wedges and fresh parsley for garnish.

(Continued on the next page)

Continued (Bush Baked Alaska Salmon)

You can't beat a dinner of fresh salmon, salad and boiled small potatoes. For dessert serve a small piece of our Rhubarb-Berry Cobbler with vanilla bean ice cream or whipped cream. Just doesn't get any better than this.

Tips: If you don't have a fresh salmon fillet, use frozen salmon and doll it up with whatever you have in the refrigerator.

Sauté onions and serve on top, use teriyaki sauce, marinate in your favorite store purchased marinade, use parmesan cheese mixed with some mayonnaise and garlic salt. Cut in chunks, make a beer batter and deep fat fry, bake in oven with basic seasoning, flake and make a frittata, or a salmon salad with store bought ranch dressing.

Salmon is an extremely versatile fish and can be fixed in a multitude of ways. **Caution - you can ruin your dish by overcooking the salmon, so watch it carefully.**

Salmon Fun Fact:

There are five species of salmon in Alaska. They are born in fresh water and migrate to sea, returning to fresh water to reproduce (spawn). The size, color and characteristics of salmon vary and the colors change as they migrate from fresh water to sea water. Beaver ponds are great habitats for juvenile salmon.

Homer Pretzel (Fish) Fingers

As commercial fishermen, we always asked for these treats!

Ingredients
- 1 pound of bite size fingers of halibut (any white fish is great)
- 1 bag of salted pretzels, sticks are best, but any will be yummy
- 2 eggs
- 1 cup flour
- oil to quickly fry
- large frying pan

Directions
Prepare fish with no skin and all bones removed into long finger bite size pieces.

Crush the bag of pretzels into small course pieces inside a clear bag.

In three separate bowls, add the following and roll the fish fingers into the mixes in this order:
- 1st bowl flour
- 2nd bowl eggs beaten into a froth
- 3rd bowl crushed pretzels

Heat the oil in your frying pan until 350 degrees or a dot of water dances when dropped in oil. Always be careful with hot oil.....Do not be distracted as this should be a fast process. Gently place each fish finger into the oil, watch till brown and then turn over to other side. Brown then gently place on paper towel lined sheet pans to drain and rest. Cover.

When all fingers are complete place into a warm 200-degree oven as you prepare to plate or serve.

Accompany these delicious fish fingers with the Russian River Raspberry Slaw, and of course the Alaska Fried Rice recipe to complete your presentation. Garnish, garnish!

FIVE FINGERS UP!

Kasilof King Salmon Patty Burgers

If you are trying to eat a healthy diet, add more fish to your menu. These salmon burgers are a delight any night of the week and served on a fresh onion roll, wrapped in lettuce or just served out of the pan are sure to please any palate.

Serves 4

Ingredients
- 2 cups flaked cooked salmon, no skin and pin bones removed
- 6 green onions chopped, including tops
- 2 eggs
- 12 saltines crushed or 1 cup panko or seasoned bread crumbs
- 1 tsp. garlic salt
- ½ tsp. pepper
- 1-2 tbsp. all-purpose seafood seasoning, such as Johnny's or Old Bay
- 1 4 oz. can chopped mild green chilies
- 2 tbsp. butter or canola oil for frying patties

Directions
Mix all ingredients in a medium size bowl. If you use more salmon to increase the number of patties, add another egg so the mixture will not be too dry. Form into burger-sized patties. Fry on medium heat in the pan, approximately 5-7 minutes per side, depending on the size of your patty.

Serve with a green salad or our Russian River raspberry slaw.

Tip: If you would like a little zing, add a dash of your favorite hot sauce or a little horseradish.

Seward Peninsula Seafood Tacos

A great way to infuse Tuesday 'Taco-Time' for the Kidz with healthy fish.

Serves 4-6

Ingredients

- 2 tbsp. canola oil for frying fish
- ½ cup mayonnaise
- ½ cup Dijon/garlic-mustard (Aioli) dressing with seasoning. *
- 1 lb. of halibut or other white fish such as cod
- 4 tbsp. seasoned flour
- mixed cabbage colors or carrot coleslaw
- garnish with lime or cilantro
- taco shells- purchased, corn or flour - see note.

Directions

Ready a deep pan with 2 tbsp. canola oil. Heat to 350 degrees.

Make coleslaw and add mixture of mayonnaise or mustard/garlic Aioli *. Add your own spices.

Fillet the halibut to bite size pieces, cut against grain and take out any visible bones. Roll the fish in flour mixture and quickly fry pieces until brown.

Fill warmed taco shells with coleslaw and add warm pieces of halibut gently to shell. Add a dollop of aioli dressing on top and garnish with a lime wedge or cilantro or fruit.

Note: *Using the fresh flour and corn tortillas offers a homey semi-crunch taco shell.*

There are several ways to form the bowl of a shell, either from the oven or fry.

When in oven, lightly spray each tortilla with oil or butter and lay over oven-proof bowls or edges at 90 degrees. Bake at 350 degrees until lightly brown and taco firmly folded.

If frying, place a large metal spoon inside each tortilla and quickly brown in skillet at 90 degrees on each side.

Bueno Tacos!

ALASKA'S 49 FLAVORITE RECIPES

'Alcan' Flat Tire Crêpes
(Alaska-Canadian Highway)

So many ways to say, is it a pancake or crêpe? Yummers! Tasty and easy for the Bakery, Dessert and even Kidz Korner.
Serves 4-6 after filling

Ingredients

In Blender:

- 1 cup flour
- 3 large eggs whipped
- 2 tsp. vanilla
- 1 tbsp. heaping white sugar
- 1/8 tsp. table salt
- 1 cup warm milk
- 1 tbsp. butter per pancake to fry

- Powdered sugar to sprinkle and dust
- Flavorite jams, jellies, honey, peanut butter, whipped cream or even ice cream.
- Be creative on all the different fillings, nuts, or M&M's?

Directions

Mix all ingredients in the blender. Should look like pancake batter.

Heat your skillet with butter and pour batter enough to fill bottom as it puffs around the edges. Cook till brown and edges curve up.

Or, serve individually as you fill with favorite peanut butter, Nutella, ice cream, whipped cream, fresh berries and let your taste buds go wild.

Making smaller crêpes, ask guests to fill their own. Nuts, of course, or go completely off course and be Mexican and make a taco with all the accoutrements. Sassy and delicious.

Flat tires are full and Let's Eat!

Note: *A large cast iron skillet works best. May use non-stick skillet too.*

Berry Nice Scones

Scones are a nice change from the traditional muffin or bread served with your breakfast menu, or just to enjoy during the day with a cup of hot coffee. Easy to make or make days ahead and throw in your freezer for unexpected company.

Bake at 400 degrees for approximately 15 minutes

Ingredients
- 3 cups flour
- ½ cup sugar
- 1 ½ tsp. salt
- 1 ½ tsp. baking soda
- ½ cup butter chopped into small pieces
- 1 cup buttermilk
- 1 cup blueberries, chopped strawberries, chopped blackberries, chopped cranberries or craisins
- Zest from a lemon or orange

Directions
Mix flour, sugar, salt and baking soda together in a small bowl. Cut butter into flour mixture with a knife until you have small pea size pieces. Add chopped fruit carefully so as not to change color of the dough. Add buttermilk and gently knead until the dough is barely incorporated. May need to add a little more buttermilk. Be careful not to overmix, or dough will become tough. Place dough in an 8 or 9-inch cake pan that has been sprayed with a non-stick spray. Spray your hands with non-stick spray and gently spread to the edge of the pan. Bake at 400 degrees for approximately 15 minutes or until done. Cut into 12 pie slice shaped pieces.

Note: If you don't have buttermilk, use your regular milk and add 1 tsp. vinegar or lemon juice. You can use nuts or raisins in place of fruit if you prefer.

Big Lake Blueberry Pancakes

Alaskans love blueberry pancakes. Probably because we have so many places to pick wild blueberries and low bush cranberries. When August comes you know it is time to head to check on the blueberries that dot our landscape. Wild Alaska blueberries, while not as large as domesticated blueberries, are usually sweet due to the long daylight hours in the summer months. We find many uses for blueberries but none better than blueberry pancakes.

Serves 4 Makes 16 4-inch pancakes

Ingredients
- 2 eggs
- 2 cups buttermilk
- ¼ cup oil (not olive)
- 1 ¾ cup flour
- 2 tbsp. sugar
- 2 tsp. baking powder
- 1 tsp. baking soda
- ½ tsp. salt
- 1 cup blueberries

Directions
Heat griddle to 400 degrees. Medium high if using griddle on stove. In a large bowl, beat eggs, add buttermilk and oil. Add remaining ingredients and stir until large lumps disappear. Lightly grease heated griddle. I use non-stick spray. If you don't want to add berries to batter, drop a few berries on the pancake as soon as you drop batter on grill. Use approximately ¼ cup of batter for each pancake. Bake until bubbles form on the pancake and it is brown on the side on griddle. Turn over with your spatula and bake until brown. Serve with butter and warm maple syrup. Also great with Alaskan blueberry syrup.

Note: This recipe can be doubled if making for a large group. I freeze leftover pancakes to be heated in the microwave for a quick breakfast when on the go.

'Forget-Me-Not' Biscuits

These are the best biscuits ever. We have named them after the Alaska state flower, because once you taste them, you will never forget. Add sharp cheddar cheese to the recipe which gives even more flavor.

Serves 4-5

Ingredients

- 1 stick butter (½ cup)
- 2 ½ cups flour
- 1 ½ tbsp. sugar
- 1 ½ tbsp. baking powder
- 1 ¾ cup buttermilk
- ½ cup grated sharp cheddar cheese (optional)

Directions

Melt butter and pour into an 8x8 baking dish. If you are using a glass baking dish you may use your microwave to melt butter in the pan.

In a medium bowl, mix flour, sugar and baking powder. Add buttermilk, stirring until your batter is sticky. Add cheese with the buttermilk if you want a tasty biscuit.

Pour biscuit dough into pan, on top of melted butter. Spread to the edge of your pan.

Bake for 20-25 minutes, until golden brown on top.

Note: You may add other ingredients to this biscuit, but they are best served warm with a dollop of your favorite jam or jelly on top. Left overs, if there are any, may be frozen and warmed up for dinner on another day.

Homestead English Muffins

Ahh, the aroma of fresh breads, and homemade Alaska berry jams. Life on the Kenai Peninsula meant bread making almost every day. Amazingly easy and an incredibly rewarding breakfast or a grilled sandwich classic.

Makes 12 3-4-inch muffins

Ingredients
- Large buttered glass mixing bowl
- 1 cup warm milk
- 2 tbsp. white sugar
- 1 package active dry yeast or 1 ½ tsp. yeast
- 1 cup warm water
- 2 tbsp. melted shortening or butter
- 6 cups flour
- 1 tsp. table salt
- ½ cup yellow cornmeal for dusting

Directions
In a small saucepan warm the milk and when milk bubbles form, add sugar and stir until dissolved, then cool.

In small bowl dissolve yeast in 1 cup warm water. Let rest for 10 minutes stirring until creamy.

Large bowl mix milk, yeast mixture, melted butter and 6 cups flour. Beat with mixer or by hand until dough forms a moist ball.

Place in buttered large bowl, cover and let rise until almost doubled.

While dough is rising take a large sheet pan and dust with the cornmeal.

Also flour a large sheet pan upside down and use a floured rolling pin.

(Hint, no rolling pin? Try a floured bottle or large round glass).

Take the raised dough out of bowl and punch down and roll out evenly to 1 inch thickness on your upside down floured sheet

(Continued on the next page)

pan. Cut out as many rounds as possible. Use a glass or even an empty can to cut even, same size 3-3 ½ inch circles. Place the round dough on the corn meal sheet 2 inches apart. Cover and turn over onto cornmeal sheet so both sides have been in the cornmeal. All the muffins should be at least 2 inches apart on sheet. Cover and allow to rise till doubled (about 20-30 minutes).

If you have leftover dough re-roll and cut again to the corn meal sheet. Turn on grill to 325 degrees. Spray your largest electric grill with oil. Gently lay each rounded muffin 2 inches apart on the grill. Fry 7 minutes on each side or until browned.

Place on corn meal sheet pan to cool. Also makes a great muffin pizza. Serve with your flavorite jam or jelly.

Ohhhh my, sit and bask in the compliments. What's for breakfast, lunch or dinner?

. . . .

English Muffin Fun Fact:

English muffins are not well known in England. They are grilled, not baked and were called English muffins to differentiate from the American muffin, cupcakes, etc. McDonalds has been using English muffins since 1964.

Simply Sisters
Favorite Gingerbread Loaf

I make this gingerbread loaf at Christmas, wrap in red or green cling wrap with a bow on top, and give to friends to enjoy on Christmas morning. Your friends will want a copy of this recipe to share with others. This is the best!

Serves 6-8 Bake at 350 degrees

Ingredients

- 1 ½ cups flour
- 2 tsp. cinnamon
- 1 tsp. ground cloves
- 2 ¼ tsp. ground cloves
- 1 tsp. salt
- ½ cup softened butter
- 1 egg
- 1 cup sugar
- 1 tsp. orange extract (optional)

- 1 cup unsweetened applesauce
- 1 tsp. baking soda
- Frosting
- 1 8 oz. package cream cheese softened
- 1 tsp. vanilla
- ½ tsp. orange extract
- 2 ½ cups powdered sugar

Directions

Grease and flour a 2 quart loaf pan. Mix flour, cinnamon, cloves, ginger and salt. In a medium size bowl, cream butter, egg and sugar until fluffy. Stir in orange extract. Mix baking soda in applesauce and stir into creamed mixture. Add dry ingredients and stir until flour mixture is incorporated into creamed mixture.

Bake at 350 degrees for 45 - 50 minutes.

Frost when cool. Decorate with chopped candied orange peel or chopped ginger.

Note: May use 2 medium foil loaf pans if you prefer. Spray with non-stick cooking spray with flour before filling.

Beluga Blueberry Zucchini Bread

The beluga whale or white whale can often be seen in Cook Inlet chasing salmon that are migrating to spawn in their birthplace. Beluga is also a town on the west side of the Cook Inlet, population at last count was 20.

However you choose to remember this recipe, everyone loves a warm slice of zucchini bread and this recipe brings back fond memories of that wonderful taste.

Makes 2 loaves 8x4 inches. Bake at 350 degrees for 50-60 minutes

Ingredients
- 3 eggs
- 1 cup canola or vegetable oil
- 2 cups sugar
- 3 tsp. vanilla extract
- 2 cups grated raw zucchini
- 3 cups all-purpose flour
- 1 tsp. salt, baking soda and baking powder
- 3 tsp. ground cinnamon
- 1 cup blueberries, nuts, raisins or your favorite dried fruit

Directions
Beat eggs, vanilla, oil and sugar in a large bowl. Add dry ingredients to the creamed mixture and beat for 2 minutes or until mixed well. Stir in zucchini and blueberries until they are combined. Pour batter into greased and floured loaf pans. Bake at 350 degrees for 50-60 minutes or until a toothpick inserted in the middle comes out clean.

Allow loaves to cool on their side for 20 minutes. Remove from pans and allow to cool completely.

Note: *This bread freezes well and may be kept in the refrigerator for several weeks. Of course, it will be gone before you know it.*

Octopus Dogs, Mac n Cheese, Please!

Octopus Fun Fact:
Octopuses have 3 hearts and blue blood, plus squirt ink to deter predators. Alaskan artists use this special sepia colored ink for creative Alaskan art. With 8 arms and bulbous head, they are boneless and can squeeze into or out of very tight spaces. Octopuses are very clever and intelligent.

Alaskan Kidz Quesadillas

Alaskan kidz, who live in the north, south, east or west, come home from school and are hungry. Many will make a quesadilla filled with smoked salmon, cheese and chopped green chilis. What a great way to get kidz to eat a nutritious meal as this can easily be accompanied with a green salad or fruit for dinner.

If you don't have smoked salmon but would like the snack to be healthy and filling, we suggest using ham slices, sliced apples or pears and cheese. You may substitute other deli meats to pair with the fruit and cheese.

All kidz will love this snack and will love making it themselves if you slice the fruit and leave in the fridge. So EZ to make and so healthy and nutritious!

Ingredients

- 4 10-inch flour tortillas
- 1 apple thinly sliced, or 1 pear thinly sliced or a combination of both
- 1 cup shredded cheese divided
- 4 slices of deli sliced ham or another favorite deli meat

Directions

Core and thinly slice the fruit. Dip in lemon juice to keep the fruit from turning brown or sprinkle with fruit protector.

Place one tortilla on a plate if going to melt cheese in microwave. Layer deli meats and fruit and top with half of the cheese. Place second tortilla over the fruit, cheese and deli meat combination, and pop in the microwave until cheese melts. Repeat for second quesadillas.

This may also be browned, and cheese melted in a frying pan sprayed with non-stick spray on the stove.

Adults will love this too served as an EZ dish or Bite-tizer.

Kidz Breakfast Bread Roll-Ups

What could be more fun than sharing the creative sides of your 'buddy' friends? Each friend can add their own ingredients to create their special "Bread Roll." Imagine the many additions inside, from peanut butter to honey and bananas.

Ingredients

- 4 slices of bread (any kind, we like nut grains); cut off all the crusts
- 3 large eggs
- ½ cup milk
- 1 tsp. vanilla flavoring (try orange, or chocolate)
- ½ tsp. cinnamon or nutmeg with granulated sugar
- 2 tbsp. butter, margarine or non-stick spray for the griddle
- Fillers: syrups - try your 'flavorite' syrups with peanut butter, Nutella, fruit, cream cheese, honey, pie fillings, OR?

Directions

In a 4-cup bowl mix the eggs, milk and vanilla. Use a whisk and beat until frothy.

Pour egg mixture into a large dish. Use a rolling pin or a large bottle roll flat each of the crustless bread slices. Place each flattened slice of bread on a flat surface. Place and spread all your creative fillers on each slice. Slowly and as tight as possible roll each slice of bread and place seam down on a plate. Soak bread in egg mixture, roll and coat ends. Keep turning over until each bread stick is completely soaked in egg mixture.

Heat the griddle to 350 degrees, medium hot, and melt butter or spray with non-stick spray.

Place each bread roll on the griddle side by side so as not to touch. Brown on each side until golden. Before plating roll each bread in the sugar and cinnamon mixture. Then plate, sprinkle powdered sugar over for a garnish. Serve and add ice cream or cool whip. Leftovers? Doubtful. If so, wrap up bread rolls for a late nibble & yummo. Yes, you can share with other kidz.

Do not forget, be creative, serve with fruit or a smoothie. Might even be a fun dessert. If using as a dessert, top with ice cream or whipped cream. Add that cherry on top or even sprinkles.

You will be the hero to kidz and their friends!

Kidz Flavorite Trail Mix

Who doesn't like to go hiking or on a picnic? This recipe will keep your kidz or the child in you satisfied for a long time. The kidz can help you make this before your jaunt and will be asking to make it again soon. It becomes addictive very quickly.

Serves 10-12

Ingredients
- 1 lb. package sourdough nibbler pretzels
- 2 packages white chocolate chips
- 16 oz. (2 cups) roasted peanuts
- 1 package butterscotch chips
- 1 bag M&M's

Directions
Melt chips in microwave oven or in a double boiler on stove. Be care not to burn. Add other ingredients and coat well. Cool on waxed paper. Break apart and store in small snack size baggies.

Note: This recipe will make your children the hit of the party!

. . . .

Pretzel Fun Fact:
The hard pretzel was made by accident, a batch was left in the oven too long. That was in 1600.

Trail Mix Fun Fact:
A type of snack mix that originated with the Native Americans. Today's trail mix can include dried fruit, nuts, crackers, candy or chocolate and even dried meats. Enjoyed while hiking and walking on trails.

Octopus Dogs, Mac n Cheese, Please!

Kachemak Bay is home to the 'Sepia Ink' Critters. Check this out, fun and yummy!

Ingredients
- 4-6 large hot dogs
- 1 box Mac n Cheese
- 1 cup of favorite frozen peas and carrots
- Yellow mustard
- Oyster shaped crackers

Directions
Take each hot dog and place in front of you sideways. Carefully, with a small knife, 1 inch from the top, slice the rest of the hot dog in half, roll, slice in half, roll creating a total of eight legs. Continue the same process on the rest of the hot dogs.

Place each sliced 8 dog legs in saucepan cover with water and bring to a boil (about 5 minutes).

Turn off the heat and allow the dogs to rest in the pan of hot water off the stove.

Prepare the Mac-N-Cheese according to the recipe on box. Stir in frozen vegetables the last five minutes. Plate the Mac-n-Cheese nicely on a plate.

Drain all the water from Octopus dogs and arrange one or two on the top of the Mac-n-Cheese. All 8 legs should be spread out over the macaroni and spread the crackers around the plate.

Take the yellow mustard and drop a dot one for each eye, perhaps a clever smile.

Be creative. Read about Octopus and their life in the sea.

Tasty Tater-Tot-Pie for Kidz Day

Tater Tots? Adults enjoy too. Extra tots for dipping.

Serves 4-6   Bake at 450 degrees

Ingredients

- One bag (32 oz.) of Tater tots
- 1 lb. ground beef, chicken or turkey
- 1 ½ cups beef broth (or chicken)
- ¼ cup milk
- vegetables: frozen preferred: ½ cup each of peas, carrots, corn
- 3 tbsp. flour
- ¾ cup shredded cheese (mozzarella, cheddar or pepper jack)
- 1 tsp. Dijon mustard
- 1 tsp. Worcestershire sauce
- salt and pepper to taste
- ½ tsp. each: onion powder, cumin, turmeric, paprika, oregano

Directions

In a large pan, brown the ground meat with the onion powder on medium heat.

Stir until small pieces are no longer pink. Do not drain but sprinkle the flour on top and mix well into the beef. Add all the vegetables, broth and half and half milk. Stir on simmer adding the remaining spices.

Spread half of bag of tater tots on greased baking pan.

Pour all hamburger and vegetable mixture into a clear glass pie plate or 8" X 8" clear baking pan.

Sprinkle all the cheese on top of mixture. Arrange in a circle as many cooked tater tots as allowed on top of mixture in a single layer. (There may be some 'tots' left over, serve as a garnish.)

Place the uncovered dish into the heated oven and bake for 30-40 minutes.

Check pan and bake till the top of the tater-tots are browned. Serve hot with the "Tundra Tenderloin' recipe and one of our tasty salads from our cookbook.

Ooopps, eat dessert first, life is too short!

Iliamna Impossible Custard Pie

All you need to make this recipe is a blender, ingredients, and a child or adult who wants to make a delicious dessert. This recipe is so fun and simple and can be dressed up to look very fancy.

Ingredients
- 2 cups milk
- 4 large eggs
- ½ cup flour
- ½ cup sugar
- ¼ tsp. baking powder
- 1 tsp. vanilla
- 3 tsp. soft butter
- pinch of table salt
- ¼ cup sweet shredded coconut

Directions
Put all ingredients in a blender. Blend all ingredients on medium for 1 minute. Use an 8 or 9- inch glass pie pan. Spray pie pan with non-stick spray.

Be creative and sprinkle in your pie pan nuts, raisins, or even M&M's.

Pour the blended batter into the pie plate. Sprinkle liberally with flaked or shredded sweet coconut.

Bake at 400 degrees for 25-30 minutes or until a toothpick inserted comes out clean. Cool before serving.

Serve with fresh fruit slices, oh alright, ICE CREAM! Yummy! This is especially good served with an Alaska Snowball Melt cookie on the side (the recipe for that cookie is in this book).

Remember, 'Life is short, eat dessert first.'

3-2-1 Microwave Cake

Microwave Magic

Serves 2 or more ramekin size dishes about 4 inches or more.

Ingredients
- One box of angel food cake mix
- One box of chocolate cake mix (any box type of cake mix)
- Water
- 2 tbsp. if you like: nuts, raisins, dried coconut or whatever you desire
- Microwave oven

Directions
Mix the contents of the two cake mix boxes in a large zip-lock bag. Spoon 3 tbsp. of cake mix, 2 tsp. water for each ramekin size dish. Mix all together. Add options and stir.

Place in your microwave oven and cook for one minute.

Voila! You can top with ice cream or whipped cream or mix the cake up and add jam, honey or warm frostings.

Keep the rest of the cake mix in the zip lock bag for your next easy magic desserts.

3-2-1 You are Magic!

Palmer Peanut Butter Fudge

Two ingredients, 2 steps. Play Day Kidz!

Ingredients
- One jar of your flavorite peanut butter, smooth or crunchy
- One container, 15-16 oz. of ready-made vanilla frosting. Try any flavor. Be creative.
- Options - nuts, mini-marshmallows, raisins, candy or? Let your creative juices flow.

Directions
Take the lid and seal off the frosting container. Place in microwave and melt at 20 second intervals. Stir and continue melting until all frosting is a creamy consistency.

In a large bowl mix the jar of peanut butter and pour in all the melted frosting. Mix thoroughly and add any options you desire.

Pour mixture on a waxed paper-lined cookie sheet and use a spatula to spread out flat.

Chill in refrigerator for at least one hour or more.

Cut into bite size pieces and proudly say, "I made these."
Way to go Kidz!

* *

Palmer Fun Fact:
Named for the 1890s entrepreneur George W. Palmer. A trading post and later the farming town was built in today's Matanuska - Susitna Valley. Alaska's giant vegetables are famous from the Valley and late August holds the Alaska State Fair.

Yukon Chocolate Gold

You'll be very surprised by this special Alaska ingredient. Kidz play day, so easy. Do not forget to share!

Ingredients
- Makes 40-50 1-inch mounds
- 2 ½ cups of sweetened coconut, shredded
- 2 ½ cups of powdered sugar
- 1/3 cup of plain mashed potatoes (instant or regular)
- 1 cup chocolate chips (semi-sweet is best)
- 1 tbsp. soft butter
- *Optional:* Nuts, chopped - your choice, we like walnuts or pecans, chopped raisins or craisins

Directions
Take a large bowl or mixer and blend the potatoes, sugar and coconut together. Plus, options if chosen.

Form a large ball. Use a 1" melon ball scoop and form small 1-inch balls on to a wax paper lined cookie sheet. Place in refrigerator 10 minutes, to cool.

In the microwave melt the chocolate chips and butter in a small deep microwave bowl. Stir at 20 second intervals. When completely melted, dip each ball in the warm chocolate and place on waxed paper to set. Repeat until all the coconut balls are smothered in chocolate.

Hint: If your ingredients do not make tight 1-inch balls, add a small drop of water one at a time.

Place in the refrigerator for 1 hour. Serve as candy or special treats.

You can place any extras in freezer bags to have on hand. (Oops, there may not be any left!)

Alaska grown vegetables and potatoes are a statewide pride.

Yukon Spuds proudly grown in Alaska!

Check out our exciting Alaska State Fair in August of each year. See Alaskan grown pumpkins and cabbages growing to world record weights.

A-Z Alaska Geography

Alaska is the 49th State and largest state in the U.S.A. Alaska became a state on January 3, 1959, under the administration of President Dwight Eisenhower. Alaska is also the Land of the Midnight Sun, and amazing northern lights (aurora borealis). Go to the map and locate the letter with the destination.

Have fun learning A-Z Geography.
Some letters are Alaska interests and NOT on the map.

A=Anchorage, our largest city nestled on Turnagain Arm backdropped by the Chugach Mountain Range.

B=Barrow, the Inupiat name is UTQ-IAGVIK. Largest city in the North Slope Borough, above the Arctic Circle.

C=Cordova, bustling fishing community located near the mouth of the Copper River.

D=Dillingham, community on the inlet of Bristol Bay and arm of the Bering Sea.

E=Eagle River, 25 miles north of Anchorage, nestled in the Chugach Mountains on Eagle River, for which it's named.

F=Fairbanks, Alaska's second largest city, and largest in the interior of Alaska. Home of University of Alaska founded in 1917, now known as UAF.

G=Glennallen, inland community lying at the junction of the Glenn and Richardson Highways.

H=Homer, known for the Homer Natural Spit, birding, creative galleries, and seafood galore. Outstanding views of Kachemak Bay.

*I=Inuit, Group of culturally indigenous people inhabiting the Arctic regions of Greenland, Canada and Alaska.

J=Juneau, the Capital of Alaska at the base of the Alaskan panhandle. Designated in 1907 as the capital when Alaska was still a territory. Accessible only by air or sea.

K=Kodiak, off the southern coast of Alaska, is the largest fishing port, famous for catches of king crab and salmon. Also, home of the Kodiak brown bear.

*L=Lakes, Alaska boasts over 3 million lakes, many are over 20 acres each. No roads to most Alaskan lakes, they are usually reached by float planes or all-terrain vehicle.

*M=Matanuska-Susitna Borough, is the fastest growing borough in the State of Alaska. 1 hour north of Anchorage, where glaciers abound, surrounded by snow-capped peaks, and vast agricultural farming land. Palmer and Wasilla are in this borough.

N=Nome, The terminus of the famous 1,049 Mile Iditarod Dog Sled Race. Above the Arctic Circle, Nome has deep history in the Gold Rush era, 1899-1909.

N=North Pole, a town located 25 miles southeast of Fairbanks and home of Santa Claus Land.

*O=Otters, from rivers to sea, Otters are playful and curious mammals. Otter fur is the densest of any animal.

P=Palmer, Home to the Alaska State Fair, held in August. Where pumpkins weigh up to 1471.5 lbs., and cabbages 138.25 lbs. Featuring farm critters, vegetables, flower gardens, food and entertainment.

ALASKA'S 49 FLAVORITE RECIPES

P=Prudhoe Bay, in the North Slope Borough. Unofficial terminus of the Pan-American Highway. The largest oil field in North America. The first oil field was confirmed on March 12, 1968.

***Qiviut=** Kiv-ee-ute, the downy soft underwool of the Arctic musk ox. They are the finest natural fibers known to man. Near Anchorage, visit the Musk Ox and Reindeer Farms in the Mat-Su Valley.

R= Russian River, The most popular sockeye salmon stream in Alaska and top rated for rainbow trout. On the Kenai Peninsula, boasting sportsman's paradise.

S= Seward, only 2.5 hours from Anchorage, between the Kenai Mountains and waters of Kenai Fjords National Park. One of Alaska's oldest and very scenic communities.

T=Talkeetna, a quaint and adventurous town that boasts many activities. Talkeetna is nestled between Anchorage and Denali National Park and Preserve. Base for hiking expeditions and scenic Alaska flightseeing.

***U=Ulu**, all-purpose curved knife use by the Inupiat, Inuiat, Yupik and Aleut people for carving and skinning. Popular Alaska gift to be purchased from most gift shops.

V=Valdez, the southern terminus of the Alaska oil pipeline. Nestled in the Chugach Mountains with Gold Rush history, and a fishing mecca. Snowfall can annually reach over 300 inches.

W=Wasilla, the 6th largest city in Alaska and fastest growing in the state, in the Matanuska-Susitna Borough. Near mining towns, musk ox and reindeer farms.

***X= Alaska Railroad Train X-crossings**. Established in 1902, Alaska's rail system extends from Seward and Whittier, to the north as far as Fairbanks in the interior of Alaska. Trains carry both freight and passengers throughout the system all year long, including Denali National Park, for more than 471 miles.

Y= Yakutat, on a glacial moraine, surrounded by the highest coastal mountains on earth. A small resilient fishing village accessed by air or sea.

***Z= Zucchini**, in season one of the most abundant and diverse culinary vegetables of Alaska. Squash varieties can grow to as large as 70 pounds.

Find our yummy Zucchini casserole recipe in this book.

***Z= Zee end** of our Alaska geography lesson. Hope you learned something about Alaska and will share with your family and friends some facts about our state.

At the end of the line…. is your fish hook!
We hope you are HOOKED on Alaska.

Kidz Korner

KIDZ Alaska A to Z Geography

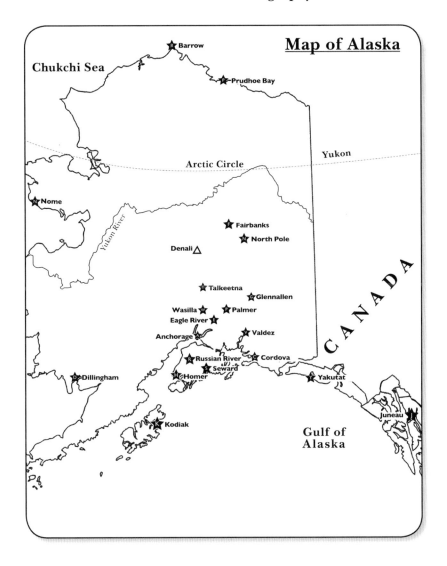

This map of Alaska only shows the A to Z geography as shown on adjacent pages.

Fun Fact: **The state of Alaska is two times larger than the state of Texas!**

Acknowledgements

This book would not have been created without the love and support of our families. We have worked on the concept and ideas for several years, but it was on a December 2017 cruise we put our thoughts on paper and knew we were ready to proceed.

We thank Judy Tymick of Big Lake, Alaska, whose thoughtful suggestions and ideas were an inspiration to our project on so many levels.

Todd Matzner is a culinary arts graduate and photographer. His photographic talents have captured the essence of our *Alaska Flavorite* recipes, as we eat, with our eyes, first.

Flip Todd of Todd Communications who met with us in July 2018 and looked at our first mock up and encouraged us to proceed with this project.

Skip and Lee Winfree, owners of 10th and M Seafoods, whose participation in this adventure is greatly appreciated.

This cookbook is dedicated to Cindy's recently deceased husband, Steve R. Smirnoff. Their vast culinary travels have been instrumental in this flavorite venture.

Additionally, John Stallone, my spouse who has always encouraged me to do something I have never done before. John is our great connoisseur in taste-testing.

Finally, we thank our parents who are no longer with us, for raising us in the great 49th State. Alaska continues to offer amazing adventures and opportunities, for all ages year around.

"Warning, We Brag about Alaska."

Simply Alaskan Sisters
Barb and Cindy